LIONEL MESSI
BIG GOALS
A BIOGRAPHY

BY **ERICA WAINER** ★ ILLUSTRATED BY **CLAUDIA MARIANNO**

HARPER
POP
An Imprint of HarperCollinsPublishers

Right now,
on any soccer field,
in any town—
small,
large,
rural,
suburban,
in the city,
or in the country—
you'll see a child wearing this jersey.

Or maybe this one.

Or this one, too.

And after they score a goal,
they point their index fingers to the sky,
imitating the greatest soccer player of all time.

In Argentina,
when Lionel Messi was four years old
and playing soccer in his neighborhood
with his cousins and brothers,
could he have ever imagined such a thing?
Jerseys? With *his* name on them?

Even in his biggest little-kid dreams,
could Leo Messi have imagined
what life had in store for him?

Did Leo,
while playing soccer for Newell's Old Boys,
and scoring over two hundred goals
before he turned twelve,
ever think he would be
the most famous soccer player
in the entire world?

Leo was born into a soccer family.
His dad, Jorge, was his very first coach
at just four years old.

His cousins grew up to play
professional soccer.

And his grandmother Celia
took him to his practices and matches.

Young Leo was fast.

He played soccer with precision,
moving quickly up and down the pitch,
controlling the ball with ease.

But Leo was also small.

His nickname was "la Pulga"—the Flea.

He had a condition that kept him shorter than most of the kids his age.

His body didn't produce enough of the hormones needed to grow.

It was hard for his family to afford medical care that could help him.

So Leo was smaller than all of his teammates in Argentina.

Smaller than *most* soccer players anywhere.

At just thirteen years old,
the pint-sized player flew to Spain
to try out for an FC Barcelona scout.

The scout was surprised.
He thought Leo would be older.
And bigger.

The other players on the field
were all much older.
And *definitely* bigger.

But the scout had never seen anyone play like Leo.

He always had the ball.

It didn't matter how small he was.

If he lost the ball, he was relentless about getting it back.

He seemed to move even faster when he was controlling the ball.

"We have to sign him."

The story goes that Leo
signed his first professional contract
on a napkin.

He and his dad moved to
Barcelona.

And there, in Spain,
Leo was able to get
medical treatment to
help him grow a bit taller.

Leo made his debut
for the club team FC Barcelona
when he was seventeen.

He was still small,
but he was determined.

Serious.
Quiet.
Laser-focused.

His speed and explosive abilities on the field belied a shy,
reserved personality in the locker room.

Soccer meant everything to Leo.

Argentina also meant everything to Leo.
The country of his childhood,
where he fell in love with soccer,
had not won the Copa América in nearly three decades.

Even though he played professionally for the Barcelona
club in Spain, Leo wanted nothing more than to bring
the Copa América trophy to his home country.

It had been difficult to leave Argentina and play soccer
in another country.

Leo and his Argentinian national team lost in the finals three times.

2007

Brazil X Argentina
3   0

2015

Chile X Argentina
0(4)   0(1)

2016

Chile X Argentina
0(4)   0(2)

The loss in 2016 to Chile was devastating.
Leo missed a penalty kick that would have helped Argentina win.
In the locker room after the game, Leo said he was done playing
soccer for his home country.

It hurts me more than anyone, but it is evident that this is not for me. I want more than anyone to win a title with the national team, but unfortunately, it did not happen.

His retirement—thankfully—didn't last long.

And five years later,
Argentina defeated Brazil 1–0
to win the 2021 Copa América.

Leo was named the tournament's
best player,
with four goals and five assists.

Argentina would win the next Copa América, too.

By now there was no doubt that Leo Messi
was the greatest soccer player of his generation . . .
and maybe even of all time.

He is the eight-time winner
of soccer's biggest personal award,
the Ballon d'Or.

He scored the most goals (672!)
for a single football club
while he was with Barcelona.

He scored 91 goals in one year.

Off the field,
he had gotten married,
started a family,
and begun the Leo Messi Foundation
to help children of all backgrounds
realize their dreams.

Just like Leo had done.

But there was still one thing
Leo had not accomplished. . . .

Argentina had not won the FIFA World Cup since 1986,
when Argentinian soccer legend Diego Maradona
captained the team to victory.

After thirty-six years,
Argentina,
and Leo Messi,
won the World Cup.

The image of him lifting the trophy in 2022 became
the most popular
Instagram post
ever,
with over seventy-five million likes.

Leo has played for many teams
across the globe—
from his first neighborhood team in Rosario
to Barcelona,
Paris,
Argentina,
and now Miami.

Millions of fans have put on his jersey
and watched him make the game of soccer
look simple.

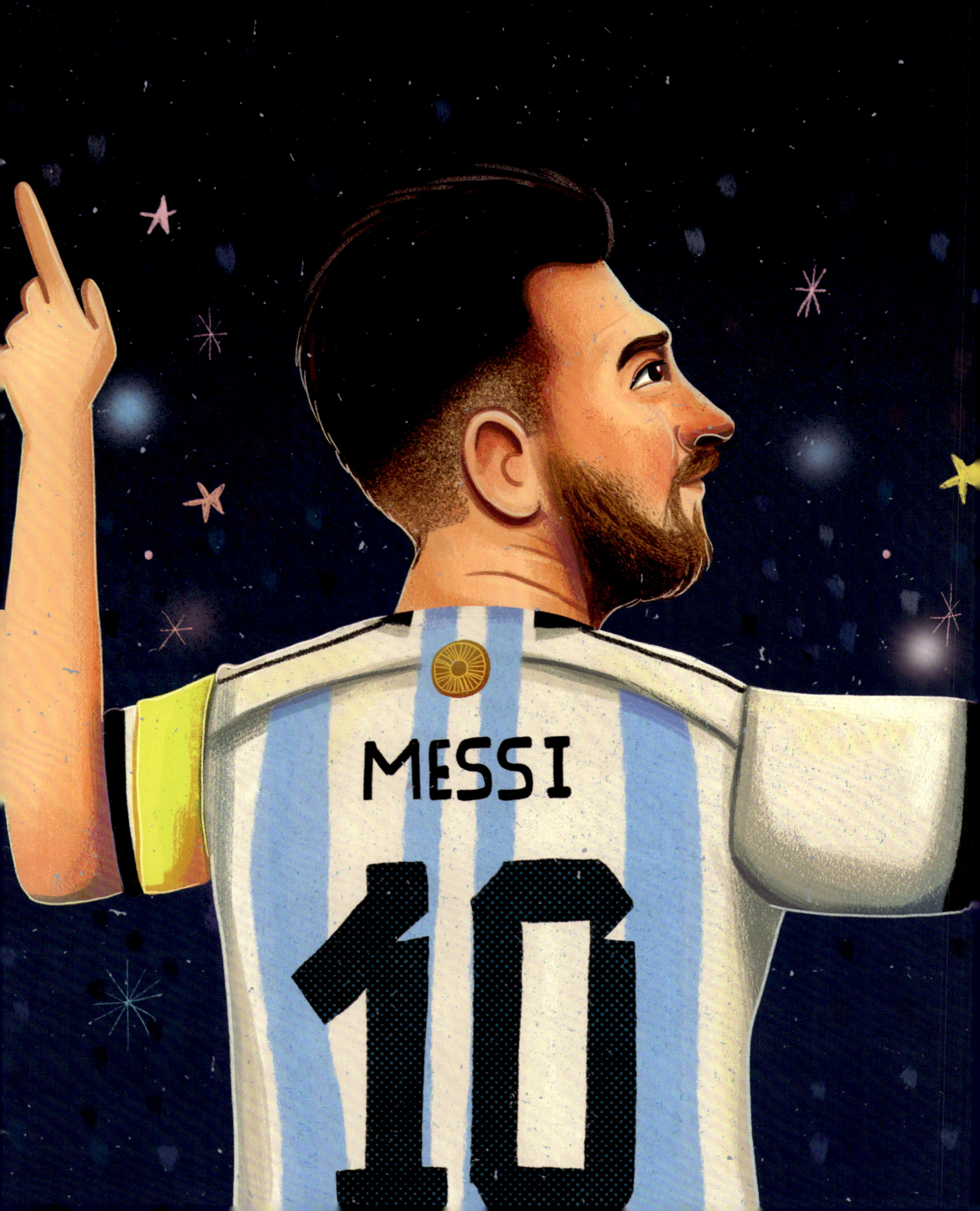
MESSI
10

Did Leo Messi ever believe
that he would be known all over the world?

Did he dream
of traveling to far-away countries,
joined by his family,
meeting with fans,
with leaders,
with children who reminded him
of himself
way back
when he was the smallest kid on the pitch?

To my friends of a lifetime
from Wakefield High School—
I love being on your team. —E.W.

For Olga,
my biggest idol —C.M.

HarperCollins Children's Books, a division of HarperCollins Publishers, 195 Broadway, New York, NY 10007

HarperCollins Publishers, Macken House, 39/40 Mayor Street Upper, Dublin 1, D01 C9W8, Ireland

HarperPop is an imprint of HarperCollins Publishers.

Lionel Messi: Big Goals: A Biography

Library of Congress Control Number: 2025946025
ISBN 978-0-06-349488-6

The artist used Photoshop to create the digital illustrations for this book.
Typography by Stephanie Hays
26 27 28 29 30 RTLO 10 9 8 7 6 5 4 3 2 1

First Edition

The quote on page 25 is taken from ESPN, "Lionel Messi Retires from Argentina."

Sources

Adán, D. "Leo Messi, the Little Boy Who Became the Greatest in History." Diario AS USA, December 7, 2022. en.as.com /soccer/lionel-messi-the-little-boy-who-became-the-greatest-in-history-n-2.

ESPN. "Lionel Messi Retires from Argentina After Copa America Final Loss to Chile." June 27, 2016. www.espn.com /soccer/story/_/id/37477184/lionel-messi-retires-argentina-copa-america-final-loss-chile.

ESPN FC. "Lionel Messi Finally Wins Copa America: Argentina Wanted It for Him." July 12, 2021. YouTube. www .youtube.com/watch?v=QI-LPpVeg3c&t=117s.

Lane, B. "Lionel Messi Facts: Amazing Things You Didn't Know About the Soccer Legend." Sports Illustrated, April 3, 2025.

Lowe, S. "Lionel Messi: How Argentinian Teenager Signed for Barcelona on a Serviette." The Guardian, October 15, 2014.

Luke, G. "Lionel Messi: From a Tumultuous Childhood to Greatest of All Time." The Highlander, March 2, 2023.

Mukherjee, S. "Why Is Lionel Messi Called 'La Pulga'? PSG Star's 'Flea' Nickname Meaning Explained." Goal.com USA, June 23, 2022. www.goal.com/en-us/news/why-lionel-messi-called-la-pulga-psg-flea-nickname-meaning -explained/bltaf91687a3d94468b.

Schneider, J. "Remember When Lionel Messi Shockingly Retired from Argentina After the 2016 Copa America Final? Yeah, We Do, Too." Goal.com USA, June 20, 2024. www.goal.com/en-us/lists/remember-lionel-messi-retired -argentina-penalty-kick-2016-copa-america/bltcd3422ba6ff97b30.

Swan, R., and C. Ritchie. "How Many Goals Lionel Messi Scored for Newell's Old Boys." GiveMeSport, February 13, 2024. www.givemesport.com/lionel-messi-goals-for -newells-old-boys.

Tony, H. "Lionel Messi: In Others' Words." Coaches' Voice, January 5, 2022. learning .coachesvoice.com/cv/lionel-messi-barcelona-paris-saint-germain.

Wikipedia. "Diego Maradona." Last modified August 17, 2025. en.wikipedia.org/wiki /Diego_Maradona.

Wikipedia. "Lionel Messi." Last modified August 17, 2025. en.wikipedia.org/wiki /Lionel_Messi.